THE BEST I CAN WITH WHAT I HAVE

God doesn't call us to perfection.
He calls us to do our best.

Heather Carroll

ISBN 979-8-89309-483-1 (Paperback)
ISBN 979-8-89309-484-8 (Digital)

Copyright © 2024 Heather Carroll
All rights reserved
First Edition

All rights reserved. No part of this publication may be reproduced, distributed, or transmitted in any form or by any means, including photocopying, recording, or other electronic or mechanical methods without the prior written permission of the publisher. For permission requests, solicit the publisher via the address below.

Covenant Books
11661 Hwy 707
Murrells Inlet, SC 29576
www.covenantbooks.com

CONTENTS

Acknowledgments v
Introduction vii

Chapter 1: We Were Created on
            Purpose and for a Purpose 1
Chapter 2: Judgment and Comparison 9
Chapter 3: We Are Called 24
Chapter 4: Purpose in Our Failings and Lack 29
Chapter 5: Grace and Mercy 38

References 43

ACKNOWLEDGMENTS

God is so good! I am grateful for the wonderful community that He has blessed me with. There have been many people who have believed in and encouraged me along this journey. I would like to specifically thank my husband, Brian, for supporting and walking down this path with me. This experience has helped us have a better understanding of each other and grow us and our relationship in many ways.

I am so grateful for my parents who have been extremely patient and loving with me. They have always believed in my capabilities despite my doubts and stubbornness. I appreciate them and how they never hesitate to support me in any way they can.

Thank you to my kids for making parenting such a joy and giving a great deal of purpose to my life. What a gift of self-reflection God has designed in the parent-child relationship. I appreciate how my kids have inspired, loved, and challenged me over the years.

There are a couple of other important recognitions that I would like to make. I would like to thank Audrey Meisner for being a mentor, inspiration, and friend. Thank you for all your nuggets of wisdom and encouragement. Also, thank you to Victorious Christian Living Institute for pushing me to follow through on what God has been calling me to for years.

INTRODUCTION

I am the wife of a wonderfully patient and brilliant man named Brian. We have five beautiful children together. My husband and I, like anyone else, ventured into this life/parenting gig one day at a time, doing the best we could with what we knew. Some of our beliefs and ideas came from our upbringings, sorting through the honorable decisions as well as the mistakes of generations before us. Other beliefs and ideas came from incorporating our observations of those around us in similar seasons of life together with our own trials and errors.

Over the years, we made many life decisions that proved themselves to be controversial. Probably the most controversial being I chose to give up a well-paying job for many minimal-paying side jobs, to forgo day care and babysitters and homeschool my kids. Likewise, my husband has said no to higher-paying jobs resulting in large amounts of travel time to ensure his participation in the family's activities. Though the journey has not been without its hurdles, God has blessed us in so many ways, and we don't regret those choices. However, we are now keenly aware of how the general population feels regarding our decisions.

We could have easily chosen to only socialize in groups of like-minded people; there is nothing wrong with that. Instead, we intentionally elected to do a hybrid version of that by inserting ourselves and our children into many mainstream places where we were able to learn, grow, and serve. Those experiences taught me many things that inspired me to write this book. I continually found myself in the presence of individuals feeling defeated or discouraged by their perceived failures and in constant cycles of judgment. I developed an intense passion for helping them overcome life's difficulties by pointing them toward God's perspective. I used God's promises as well as my personal experiences to encourage and instill hope.

The truth is, God has created us on purpose and for a purpose. We all have a calling on our lives. However, He does not call us to be perfect, He calls us to do the best we can with what we have. He offers us freedom with His grace. He lays out what perfection looks like in His son, Jesus Christ. Jesus came to accomplish what we cannot. We live in a fallen world full of sin. We, ourselves are sinners; "none is righteous, no, not one." We should not get caught up in judging or comparing ourselves to others. This book will help you see grace as the better option. God calls us to repentance and love. He wants us to repent when we recognize our actions as wrong and move forward striving to grow and do better. He wants us to love those around us by showing grace and helping them to grow; this is how we show Him our love as well. I also believe that our lack, shortcomings, and failures actually offer purpose to the lives of others. This is His purpose for them, and how "all things work together for good."

1

We Were Created on Purpose and for a Purpose

Over the years, I have found myself in many conversations with people either condemning themselves or others for not measuring up to what the world would consider to be acceptable. The problem with this is that everyone in the world has a different idea as to what "acceptable" is. What is acceptable or even obviously right to one person will be obviously wrong to another. This creates a very difficult situation for those trying to measure up.

I remember several years ago, coming across a girl broken and in a puddle of her own tears. She was a brand-new mother with an adorable baby girl. While comforting her, I listened to her sob about how she was a terrible mother. I tried to reassure her that she hadn't even had enough time to prove that yet. However, her distraught mind wouldn't absorb the encouragement I was trying to give her. She explained that one of her closest friends had seen her bottle-feeding her baby and came down pretty hard on her for it. The friend informed her that bottle-feeding wasn't the best thing for her baby; instead, nursing was the only way she would be able to create a bond. It was God's perfect milk that He created just for her daughter. It would provide her with a healthy immune system and give her body exactly what it needed. The friend proceeded to announce that she couldn't understand how anyone could ever even think of bottle-feeding and not loving their baby enough to sacrifice themselves and give them the very best.

As I spent more time listening to her, I realized the hardest part for the girl was that she had a desire to breastfeed her baby. Disappointingly, her body wasn't cooperating, and she was already struggling with her own internal dialogue of shame and doubt. The words of her friend were just solidifying them. My heart was broken for her.

THE BEST I CAN WITH WHAT I HAVE

It can be very difficult to drown out the roar of the world's perspective. As Christians, God's opinion should be the only one that matters to us. Second Corinthians 11:3 (ESV) says, "But I am afraid that as the serpent deceived Eve by his cunning, your thoughts will be led astray from a sincere and pure devotion to Christ." I believe the enemy whispers lies in our ears that amplify the actions and opinions of others, either good or bad, with the intent of causing division. These lies distract us from the purpose God has for us, planting seeds of doubt, fear, boasting, etc.

So what does God have to say about this? I believe He doesn't call us to meet a standard of perfection. I believe He calls us to do the best we can with what we have. The new mom I spoke of above was, in fact, doing the best she could with what she had. Her baby needed to eat. Her body wasn't producing what she needed to feed her. Therefore, she pivoted, making sure her baby was taken care of. God knew the struggle she was going through, and He provided another way. At a time when she should have been enjoying her precious new gift and rejoicing in God's goodness, she was distracted by the lies of the enemy, whispering to her that she wasn't a good-enough mom and that she didn't love her baby enough to sacrifice for her. She was convinced she was broken and somehow to blame for it.

This girl let the enemy get in her head and distract her from the purpose God had placed in front of her. When God created her, He knew she would have that baby. He knew she would be the one to care for her. He chose her to be a mom; to be her mom, knowing she would do the best she could with the skills, gifts, and background that she had.

Genesis 1:27 (ESV) says, "So God created man in his own image, in the image of God he created him; male and female he created them." If He created us all in His image, then why are we all so different?

We all come from different places, backgrounds, and ethnicities, with different people raising us, different ideas poured into us, different traumatic experiences in different amounts—the list goes on and on. Even those coming from the same genetic descent will have their own uniqueness. They can grow up to believe differently, think differently, and even have completely different perspectives on what it was like to grow up in the same home with the same parents. How could this be?

For years, this fact puzzled me. The truth is, each child will have different experiences even in the same home and with the same parents. The same situations will be experienced differently by each of them. Many factors play into this. They each have different roles or positions they hold in the family. They have different outside influences that played into their various viewpoints. However, I believe the most prominent factors are their personality differences, as well as the unique gifts and talents that God gave to each of them, causing them to have different abilities as well as limitations.

No matter who we are, where we are from, what we have done, what was done to us, or simply what perspective we have, our life's circumstances have shaped who we are and who we will become. They have an influence on our choices and behaviors going forward in life. Whatever our life's circumstances are, I believe God wants us to learn from them. He wants us to try to be and do better, as well as emulate the things that were positive. However, we will fall short, we will fail, and we will lack. He knows this about us, and I believe He has purpose in that too. Romans 8:28 (NIV) says, "And we know that in all things God works for the good of those who love him, who have been called according to his purpose."

So how does this play out in our daily lives? If you look a little further into the book of Romans, in 12:4–8 (ESV), it says,

> For as in one body we have many members, and the members do not all have the same function, so we, though many, are one body in Christ, and individually members one of another. Having gifts that differ according to the grace given to us, let us use them: if prophecy, in proportion to our faith; if service, in our serving; the one who teaches, in his teaching; the one who exhorts, in his exhortation; the one who contributes, in generosity; the one who leads, with zeal; the one who does acts of mercy, with cheerfulness.

We are all beautifully and wonderfully made in God's image. However, "the members do not all have the same function." This is important. Honestly, this is one of my favorite things about God's creation.

THE BEST I CAN WITH WHAT I HAVE

We are created differently with and for different purposes. We are expected to work together as one body. What a euphoric thought...

One of my favorite commentaries on this is found in Bob and Audrey Meisner's book, *My Personality Goals.* They talk about how we all have a song to sing. "Like a sheet of music, you are an organized pattern and combination of notes and rhythm. A continuum of melody that flows and vibrates with life, breath, and influence. Not so much complex, but rather unique. Our songs are all different and meant to work with each other in harmony." I love the idea that we all have different songs meant to be played in harmony with those around us. I love music. When I read this book, it made me think of how all the instruments of an orchestra work together to make a beautifully rich and full song. The individual musicians all work on perfecting their instruments and even the specific parts that they are assigned to play with that instrument. The truth is a tuba can't be a piccolo. It wouldn't even be possible for a tuba to play the piccolo's notes, let alone sound like one even if it could. It is important that the tuba player works on their role as a tuba. Now, as the instruments play on their own, they can create a great and beautiful sound. However, when they come together in harmony, they can achieve a depth and richness they are unable to achieve on their own, sounding somewhat euphoric when done well.

2

Judgment and Comparison

Unfortunately, euphoria is not what we tend to experience in this life. The world is full of ups and downs and twists and turns. We are pressed and stretched in ways that cause us to sometimes be out of tune. While we should all be rejoicing in our differences, instead it becomes easy to start comparing ourselves to others, either by thinking of ourselves as better than others or by thinking of ourselves as less than or not enough. To keep with the instrument theme, sometimes the tuba player wishes they could play the sounds of the piccolo, or they believe the piccolo should sound like the tuba. Both ways of comparison can be destructive and do more harm for the kingdom than good. A tuba cannot be a piccolo, nor should it be. It was created to make beautiful tuba sounds.

Second Corinthians 10:12 (ESV) says, "Not that we dare to classify or compare ourselves with some of those who are commending themselves. But when they measure themselves by one another and compare themselves with one another, they are without understanding." The King James version says, "Not wise."

Though no one likes it when people play the game of comparison, we will all likely fall into it at some point in our lives. It's difficult to stay away from. I do find it interesting that, when referring to the subject of comparing ourselves to others, the Bible would use phrases like "without understanding" or "not wise." What is it that we don't understand? Why are we "not wise"?

In 2006, I was new to homeschooling. Our co-op group had a park meetup every Friday. I remember being at the park; my sister and her six-month-old baby were with me. During this season of life, my sister was living with me so I could help her and her baby. She had had a huge medical situation surrounding the birth of her baby and required a lot of assistance. She had been through quite an ordeal but had also come a long way in her recovery, and to most people outside the situation, she appeared to be fairly normal.

This particular day started out like many fall days in Arizona, sunny, with an ideal temperature. My sister was hanging out in the mom circle while I was off chasing my one-year-old around the playground. It suddenly clouded up and got a little chilly. I heard my sister's baby fussing. The fussiness had gone on for a little bit, so I made my way over to the mom circle to see if she needed any help. As I approached, I witnessed another mother verbally chastising my sister, accusing her of being a selfish and bad mother. Her reasoning was that my sister had put a sweatshirt on herself because she was cold but had ignored her baby and not put a jacket on him also. She continued for several minutes, loudly, for all to hear. She explained she had never seen anything so appalling. I think this woman somehow thought that she could shame my sister into putting a jacket on her baby. That was not what happened. My sister did not put a jacket on him; she also didn't retaliate. She didn't say anything. She sat quietly, intimidated, and unable to even process what was being hurled at her. Of course, I grabbed his jacket and helped her put it on. I then asked the other woman to please stop and told her that there were many things she didn't understand.

The awkwardness of the moment died down and we moved on. This is a great example of being "without understanding." Though the woman was very unkind in her delivery, my sister did appear to be putting herself first or even neglecting her baby. In reality, she was, in fact, doing that. However, there was more to this situation that this woman was unaware of. My sister had experienced extreme trauma to her body and brain at the time of her son's birth. This resulted in my sister being in a coma for two weeks. The results of the coma left her continuing to have many seizures daily. Her brain was still at a place of just trying to survive and remember how to keep her own body functioning. The doctors explained to us that my sister's brain would naturally choose to focus on her body's health and continue to fight to recover. He warned us that because of this, she would not have the normal "motherly instincts" that most women have, at least not for a long while. She was struggling to think outside herself at all, even when compared with regular humans, let alone as moms think of their babies. If the other mom had known all the details of the situation, she might have (hopefully) responded differently.

THE BEST I CAN WITH WHAT I HAVE

I realize this is an extreme example, but the truth is, we make judgments on people without understanding all the time. How many of us experience bad drivers? Are we quick to judge them, or do we first consider there might be circumstances we can't or don't understand, which influence the situation?

I used to get so irritated with the people who ride out a merging lane past the place of merge, continuing to pass the other cars and force their way in. There was a day I happened to be in this situation. I was quick to judge the other driver as selfish, considering their time as more important than my own. Then a few minutes later, while still distracted by these thoughts, I somehow missed seeing a merge sign. You guessed it, soon I was driving to the right of traffic with no lane of my own. I wasn't intentionally being a nuisance; it was an honest mistake. The other drivers were very annoyed with me. To them, it looked like I had acted selfishly. I was trying to give smiles and facial expressions of apology the best I knew how, as I inserted myself into their lane. I wanted them to understand it was an accident and to forgive me for my mistake. However, they still seemed annoyed and frustrated. The truth was, they didn't have understanding.

In reality, there are plenty of drivers who are inconsiderate. They have selfishly justified their actions because they are running late, are tired of being in traffic, etc. But likewise, there are also people who maybe just made a neglectful mistake and need grace or have a legitimate reason for being in a hurry.

We can't possibly know all the reasons why people make the choices that they do, which makes us "without understanding." To judge someone without understanding is "not wise." I believe most of us have encounters with people and judge them without understanding or even attempting to understand their situations on a daily basis. We see them as not being or doing enough, or simply doing things wrong (ultimately, elevating ourselves as better than them).

Is it true that some people are selfish and unkind? Of course. Can people be wrong and completely guilty? Yes. In my case of neglecting to merge, I was definitely guilty. However, sometimes we are not acting selfishly, as it would seem. Sometimes we are just doing our best to survive. Sometimes we have a justifiable reason for our behavior. Sometimes we are sorry and need forgiveness. Whatever the case,

THE BEST I CAN WITH WHAT I HAVE

God has an opinion about how we are to respond. Colossians 3:12–15 (ESV) says,

> Put on then, as God's chosen ones, holy and beloved, compassionate hearts, kindness, humility, meekness, and patience, bearing with one another and, if one has a complaint against another, forgiving each other; as the Lord has forgiven you, so you also must forgive. And above all these put on love, which binds everything together in perfect harmony. And let the peace of Christ rule in your hearts, to which indeed you were called in one body. And be thankful.

And Ephesians 4:2 (NLT) says, "Always be humble and gentle. Be patient with each other, making allowance for each other's faults because of your love."

Like I mentioned earlier, we can also get caught up in feeling we are not enough or that we are failures, believing others to be superior to us or even perfect. Just like we don't have all the details as to why people do wrong or do things of which we disapprove, we also don't have, or sometimes simply overlook, the details of the person's life that appears to be better than us. How many of us could name a public figure or a religious leader who was seemingly wonderful and taught us many wonderful things? Then we find out later, in the details of their personal life, that they behaved unethically. There was only one man who was without blame. Everyone else will disappoint us, no matter how righteous or amazing they appear. Why, then, can we still be so hard on ourselves? We know no one is perfect, yet we often decide that others have the perfect marriage, perfect children, perfect career, etc.

I remember being in a conversation with two very close friends. These ladies were around myself and my family very often. We talked all the time. We were close enough to call each other family. We had journeyed together through many seasons of life: kid issues, health issues, you name it. In a particular conversation, one of the ladies shared a struggle she was going through with her husband. We listened intently. I had recently struggled similarly with my husband and could relate to her pain. When she was through, I shared my experience. I shared my pain, my confusion, and my emotions. I was real and raw with them. While I spoke, I was keeping busy with my hands and not looking at their faces. As I finished, I looked up. Both of their faces looked like they were in complete shock with their mouths agape.

There was an awkward moment of silence, until I asked, "What?" They explained to me they didn't think my husband and I ever had problems. They thought we had the "perfect" marriage and always got along. They said they would have never guessed we had gone through anything like this. I was so confused by their words. I had, on several occasions, asked for prayer for us as we went through things. I didn't share the details of what was going on, but I had definitely shared with them that we were struggling.

I reminded them that no one has a perfect marriage. To which they responded, "Well, we know, but we never see you and Brian fighting or not getting along. We just assumed you meant something small was going on, like…" They then proceeded to list a few insignificant, minor offenses. They even said they sometimes hadn't shared the struggles they were going through because they didn't think I could relate or understand.

I was completely blown away by this. They were correct. My husband and I didn't fight much at all, especially not in front of people. But just because we weren't screaming and yelling at each other didn't mean we were okay. The truth was, my husband and I were collapsing. Our struggle looked a whole lot more like him being silent and not speaking to me at all while I went into a deep depression and waited for him to engage. During the situation I'm referring to, Brian didn't engage for over a year. Sometimes, the pain poured out in my demeanor, usually taking the form of bitterness, disdain, and/or contempt in my tone of voice. Occasionally, this happened in public, which I thought looked like a billboard of dysfunction, with me portrayed as a monster and my husband appearing as a whipped puppy.

I thought I had been honest with them. I thought it was blatantly obvious to the whole world that we were crumbling. So how could they still believe we had the perfect marriage? I used the word *struggling*. I wasn't trying to be fake or appear perfect. It is true I didn't badmouth my husband to everyone; I tried to respect him as much as possible. We didn't have public displays of confrontation; we avoided them so as not to make others uncomfortable. And every day, in an attempt to survive, I got up, got dressed, found things to be joyful about, and tried my best to function. To some, this might look like perfection, but that would be a gross misinterpretation of what was really going on.

I often hear comments that people on social media are fake and only display the happy things. These critics believe that people want to appear perfect to the rest of the world and conceal their dysfunction. There are, of course, cases where that assessment may be accurate, but why are we so quick to judge? People on social media have a history of responding to others in harsh judgment and they're fairly brutal in the process. Many people who otherwise wouldn't (in a face-to-face situation) use those platforms to speak their opinions freely without care or concern for others' feelings. I posted a story once about how I was painting my living room. I turned around to find my two-year-old elbow deep in the paint can. I explained in my post that I was grateful my daughter was close and saved the situation from being worse than it was. Immediately, I had two different women accuse me of child neglect. They completely attacked me for being irresponsible and setting my son up to have possibly died. I was aware of my mistake. I didn't need their parenting advice or punishment to help with the situation. I quickly realized that social media was unsafe for my personal stories. I have enough trouble fighting off my inner critic and measuring up to my own standards; I couldn't possibly manage everyone else's also. My response to that situation was to not post those kinds of personal things going forward. I tend to stick to fun kid pictures and achievements that grandmas desire to see, along with prayer requests and praise reports. Some may call that fake. It isn't real, that's for sure. But social media isn't real life. In my mind, I think of it more as a type of bulletin board, in a sense, just a place for some displays and a communication tool. My intention is not to hide or portray a "perfect" life. I just feel like if you want to know my real life, then let's do real life together. Those are my personal thoughts about social media and my choices. Others may withhold details of their lives for different reasons.

I believe wisdom would suggest we should "be patient with each other, making allowance for each other's faults because of our love." People who post their beautiful family photos might, in fact, be going through a great season of life. And even if they're falling apart in real life, family photos are people displayed at their best. No one would pay for photos of everyone fighting, scowling, crying, etc. I believe most people would love to hold on to and cherish the

THE BEST I CAN WITH WHAT I HAVE

moment they shared a smile together, even if ordered to do so by a photographer. That person may also be in a low place and be searching for public validation. Although I doubt validation is what they will receive and their actions may instead prove to be fatalistic, the point is that we don't understand their motives. I consider it probable that those making the accusations of others portraying a fake life might, in fact, be internally struggling with their own inner critic telling them they don't measure up or they have somehow failed in their own life.

There are times when we feel justified in our self-deprecating thoughts, especially if we know we didn't do what we should have or didn't try our best. This could be due to unrealistic expectations of ourselves or what our gifts actually are. We could also be judging others' gifts or deeds as more important or significant than our own. Some individuals may have giftings that are naturally more publicly displayed, which doesn't make them more necessary or significant. Also, these thoughts might be created out of our own guilt if we know we haven't done our best or tried our hardest. Like I addressed earlier, we all fall short. Sometimes we don't do our best. Sometimes we are lazy or complacent. Sometimes we act out of fear or emotion. Whatever the case may be, this is not justification for comparing ourselves to others.

If you are a Christian, you know we are free in Christ. He gave his life as the punishment for our shortcomings. God would much rather see us turn our situation around by coming closer to Him and seeking His path for our lives. He wants us to get back on track by repenting and living up to our potential going forward. Hopefully, we are striving to do the best we can with what we have and know. This means we are trying to replicate the healthy things and not repeat our mistakes or the mistakes of others.

I want to challenge you to take a few minutes to search yourself. Is there an area where you have not done your best? Repent and apologize where needed. There is redemption through Christ. He meets us where we are. He is willing and able to forgive and offer healing and hope for the most hopeless of situations. It's not too late to turn it around.

According to Galatians 6:4 (NIV), "Each one should test their own actions. Then they can take pride in themselves alone, without comparing themselves to someone else." Theodore Roosevelt said, "Comparison is the thief of joy." It is hard to find the joy in our own lives when we are in constant judgment of ourselves and/or others. Don't let it steal your joy. God is the only one with the wisdom and understanding to judge those around us. Our focus should be on our own journey. Let's strive to use our gifts to work together with others and their gifts to love God's people and bring Him glory. We can celebrate our differences and rejoice in the fact that we each have something different to offer toward the mission.

This does not, however, take away the importance of learning wisdom from those that have gone before us. Let's listen to the wisdom of those on the other side of our season. We have a lot to learn from their achievements and mistakes. Proverbs 18:15 (MSG) says, "Wise men and women are always learning, always listening for fresh insights." We all need to be careful not to compare ourselves to others and always weigh what others have to offer against God's word. Learn from others—their good and their bad. Let's strive to do the best we can with what we have.

3

We Are Called

Every year Jesus' parents went to Jerusalem for the Festival of the Passover. When he was twelve years old, they went up to the festival, according to the custom. After the festival was over, while his parents were returning home, the boy Jesus stayed behind in Jerusalem, but they were unaware of it. Thinking he was in their company, they traveled on for a day. Then they began looking for him among

THE BEST I CAN WITH WHAT I HAVE

> their relatives and friends. When they did not find him, they went back to Jerusalem to look for him. After three days they found him in the temple courts, sitting among the teachers, listening to them and asking them questions. Everyone who heard him was amazed at his understanding and his answers. When his parents saw him, they were astonished. His mother said to him, "Son, why have you treated us like this? Your father and I have been anxiously searching for you." (Luke 2:41–48 NIV)

Some of you might need to read this passage from Luke a couple of times.

How do you feel when you read this passage? What thoughts come to mind? I think it is safe to say we probably aren't concerned about Jesus since we know who He is, and we know the end of the story. But how do you feel about these parents? They lost their son for three days. They didn't even know he was missing for a whole day. We've all heard the stories on the news about parents neglecting their children. How many of us have judged them? How many of us have judged parents we know, maybe even friends or family members? How many can relate to these parents, having made your own mistakes like these? Maybe you find yourself stuck in an endless cycle of self-judgment?

After three days of Joseph and Mary anxiously searching for Jesus, I can imagine how their hearts must have felt. I am sure they went through many stages of emotions. They were likely concerned for his well-being. I know he was Jesus, but God Himself entrusted them with his life. They may have felt like they had completely failed the significant task they'd been given. They may have been frustrated. Joseph may have missed three days of work that he couldn't afford to miss. These things we don't know. We only know they were "anxiously" searching, and yet when they did find him, they blamed him, as though he had intentionally hurt them.

As a parent, this scripture does a couple of things for me. It reminds me that I am not the only parent that makes mistakes. It also reminds me that God is the perfect Father, and He doesn't make mistakes. He knows I will make them, and He calls me into parenthood anyway.

Joseph and Mary were called to be parents. God knew they would not be perfect, and He still chose them for His purpose. I love that this passage is put in the Bible. I need to remember sometimes that God knows I am human, and my humanness does not disqualify me from fulfilling His purposes for my life. I am still called!

If you are a parent, God has called you to nurture, care for, love, and train another human being. That human being isn't Jesus, of course. However, it is a human being God created. He was active and present in your womb with your child, knitting together their cells (Psalm 139:13). He knows all the hairs on their head (Luke 12:7). He loves them more than you do (Ephesians 3:18–19), enough to die for them. He has entrusted you with them, to make an impact on them and to influence them. The gravity of these truths can be overwhelming for sure.

We are not all called to the same things. Even if several of us are called to be parents, our children have different needs. We are called to parent them in different ways through the different seasons of their lives. We are called differently to different things, sometimes multiple things, during different seasons of life. What I am certain of is that we all have a purpose. We are all called to be a part of His orchestra, working together in harmony with others. As members of the body of Christ, we are not called to do more than we are capable of doing. We are not capable of doing everything or being perfect. When we miss the mark, we are expected to adjust and keep moving forward. We are called to come alongside others and be patient, encouraging them and making allowances for their faults. We are called to do the best we can with what we have. What we have includes our gifts and talents we have received from God. This includes our faults, triggers due to traumas, areas we are lacking, and failings along our journey.

4

Purpose in Our Failings and Lack

We have an ongoing joke around my house regarding my "Mother of the Year" trophies. Each one of these trophies was earned, not by me being the best mother in the world but by falling short and failing. They are reminders to me and my children that I am not perfect, I don't have all the answers, and I continue to fall short. They were each hard-earned with humility, apologies, and repentance—some even having tears attached.

These fictitious trophies rest on an imaginary shelf in my mind. I'd love for them to stay there up high, out of the way to be forever forgotten. However, I believe God has a purpose in our failings also, working them all together for the good of those who love Him. When the Spirit leads me, I take those trophies down, dust them off (okay, if I am being honest, some haven't been there long enough to collect dust yet), and share them. If I see another parent feeling self-defeated, thinking they have completely failed, I hope that one of my stories might help them to feel comforted and/or hopeful. At the very least, maybe they will not feel alone on their journey. There are also those times when the Spirit leads me to share one with a parent that I hear shaming another parent for their inadequacy or failings. It is important to me that the judgmental parent understands they are in the presence of another parent who perhaps doesn't measure up to their level of expectation. Sometimes, these trophies simply serve as reminders to me of where I have been, where God has brought me, and that I am still on the journey.

Many of us will criticize others, including (and probably most of all) ourselves. If you are a parent and you have children out of diapers, chances are pretty good you have experienced your child's disapproval of your parenting choices at one time or another. Their perception can be distorted through the lenses of a child's lack of understanding, but there is also a chance it might be accurate.

I remember one of my kids explaining to me one day how I had failed them. They were right; I had missed the mark for sure. It wasn't a serious enough situation to earn me one of my trophies, which freed us up to have a lighthearted conversation. I owned my wrongdoing and apologized, but this didn't seem to be enough to satisfy their injustice. They were somewhat stuck on my shortcomings and couldn't let them go. Finally, I just told them, "What I know is this: God gave you to me. He knew who He was giving you to. He knew I wouldn't be perfect. He knew all the ways I would mess up and let you down. But I trust Him. I trust He will either fill in the gaps where I am deficient or provide for your therapy. One way or another, I'm confident that He's got you." I'm not going to lie; I made this statement flippantly because I was at a loss for what to say. Nothing seemed to be enough. I hadn't thought through the truth that it entailed. It did create a break in the conversation and cause my child to laugh out loud, relieving us both of the seemingly endless cycle we were in.

This statement rang in my head, echoing on for days. I meditated on it. It is true; God did know me and my shortcomings before He made me a mother.

He knew when and how I would fail, and yet He still called me to parenthood. The truth is, I am not enough. I can't do it on my own. I could sure try, but I am certain it isn't what is best for any of us.

We must trust that God will fill in the gaps. My "Mother of the Year" trophies and my faults and failings have purpose, so do the areas where I am deficient, my "gaps." The truth is where I am deficient, another has; where I fail, another succeeds; and where I struggle, another has overcome. This is how we experience the harmony in life. If I was gifted in every area or succeeded in everything I did, I would have no need for anyone else. Most of all, I would have no need for God. There are so many purposes in our lack. The purpose in my own life is that each hard-earned trophy will help me remain humble. It builds my faith as I experience God filling in and draws me closer to Him in my time of need.

I was pregnant with my fifth child in 2009 while the economy was in a severe decline. My husband, who works in the construction industry, worked for a small private company that ultimately did not survive. Work for him was sparse, often having long periods of time without. He ended up having to find a new job that did not pay as well. We were in a serious financial crisis, and I was pregnant. I began having contractions very early on that couldn't be controlled, and I was put on bed rest for the remaining four months of my pregnancy. This was around the same time the bank issued us a foreclosure notice with a date stamped on it that was one day after my due date. At that time, the banks were giving families as little as three days to get out of their homes before they locked them out. What we were lacking in money and resources, we had accumulated in stress. The worst part was that I felt fine, but I had to sit and watch my husband carry this load on his own. For added fun, he got the swine flu in the middle of this ordeal and at some point, started having heart attack symptoms that proved to be anxiety from the stress. Needless to say, we were lacking in so many ways and had gaps everywhere we turned. But...God is good! All the time! And all the time, God is good! He showed up in a big way, and He wasn't even subtle about it.

The first way He showed up was through my sister-in-law. My brother's family was in the process of moving at the time it all started and had asked if they could stay at our house until they found a place of their own to live. The day they had to be out of their house was the same day I was put on bed rest. They received the keys to their new place the very day I had my son, which was not planned. My sister-in-law, with four small children of her own in tow, took care of me and my kids every single day. She bathed my kids, fed all of us, reinforced my bed rest orders (I'm not a very compliant patient), and tended to any needs we had. She did all this happily with a faithful and grateful heart. There was also a wonderful community of people who gathered around us. They brought us food, picked up my kids and took them to their activities so they didn't have to miss out, packed up my house, sat with me and played cards, helped my husband pack and move things into storage, as well as prayed for us daily. My parents even purchased a house we could rent from them, so we had a place to go. We absolutely could not have made it through that time without God sending in His saints to fill in where we were deficient. It drew us closer to Him and reminded us of all the things we had to be thankful for every single day. He showed up in the form of many friends and family.

Beyond being used to humble ourselves, encourage others, and show us our need for God, our shortcomings, failings, and/or struggles give purpose to others' lives as well. We are all called to get outside ourselves and love others by serving, comforting, encouraging, etc. Our opportunities to

THE BEST I CAN WITH WHAT I HAVE

fulfill our purposes are made available because others have fallen, struggled, or are in need. In Jesus's time on Earth, He made this very clear. In Matthew 22:34–39 (ESV), when the Pharisee asked Jesus what the greatest commandment was, He answered, "You shall love the Lord your God with all your heart and with all your soul and with all your mind. This is the great and first commandment. And a second is like it: You shall love your neighbor as yourself." In Luke 10, when that same man asked Jesus to define who his neighbor was, Jesus told him the parable of the good Samaritan. This is a story about a man who was robbed, beaten, and left for dead on the road. Two men, a priest and a Levite (religious leaders under God's law) saw him on the road but went out of their way to go around him. The third man, a Samaritan, stopped to bind and clean the man's wounds and get him to help, even sacrificing his own money to pay for his treatment. Jesus states in Luke 10:37, the one who proved to be the neighbor of the hurt man was "the one who showed him mercy." Then He told the Pharisee to "go and do likewise." It is clear that God has called us to love Him and love others. This is the core of everyone's purpose.

Just as our purpose of loving others can be found by coming alongside those who have failed or struggled, we can also fill our purpose of loving God in the same way. In Matthew 25:35–40 (ESV), when Jesus speaks of the final days of judgment and who will inherit the Kingdom of Heaven, he tells his disciples,

> "For I was hungry and you gave me food, I was thirsty and you gave me drink, I was a stranger and you welcomed me, I was naked and you clothed me, I was sick and you visited me, I was in prison and you came to me." Then the righteous will answer him, saying, "Lord, when did we see you hungry and feed you, or thirsty and give you drink? And when did we see you a stranger and welcome you, or naked and clothe you? And when did we see you sick or in prison and visit you?" And the King will answer them, "Truly, I say to you, as you did it to one of the least of these my brothers, you did it to me."

THE BEST I CAN WITH WHAT I HAVE

When we give of ourselves and love those around us, we are not just loving them, we're also showing love to God our Father. As a parent myself, I can understand this. When I was on bed rest, though I enjoyed friends that came over to hang out and keep me company, the most loving thing I experienced, without a doubt, was when people showed up to help my husband and love my kids the way I desired to love them. Likewise, when someone hurts my husband or my children, it also hurts me. God is love, and He loves us even more than we are capable of loving our own children. When we set out to serve and love Him, He cares deeply about the level of grace and mercy we show His other children.

5

Grace and Mercy

It is important to recognize that we are not perfect. No matter our efforts, we will never get there on this side of heaven. It is also important to understand how God can work all our imperfections together for our good, for our purpose, and ultimately His purpose. To go back to our earlier analogy of an orchestra, if we were all perfect and didn't need each other, we would all be playing solos. Since we are all so different, this would be a different song for everyone, all playing at the same time. I would not buy tickets to that concert. There is so much beauty and purpose in the harmonies created by God.

THE BEST I CAN WITH WHAT I HAVE

Each of us was created on purpose and for a purpose. Ephesians 2:10 (ESV) says, "For we are His workmanship, created in Christ Jesus for good works, which God prepared beforehand, that we should walk in them." First Peter 4:10 (ESV) says, "As each has received a gift, use it to serve one another, as good stewards of God's varied grace."

All that considered, remember, we have been called to be a part of something great. When we are distracted and caught in the judgment and comparison cycle or self-loathing, it becomes difficult to participate in the great purpose God has for us. He doesn't expect us to be perfect. He expects us to do the best we can with what we have. We have not been accepted into His orchestra based on our abilities or because of how great we are. We are accepted because Christ's death on the cross made us acceptable. When we fail or fall short, we are not disqualified from participating in His great plan. Contrarily, we are accepted in spite of our actions and, instead, expected to participate using those failings and shortcomings in conjunction with our giftings for His plan.

He knows who we are, where we came from, what gifts, as well as what deficiencies we possess; and He has still called us. He has offered His grace to us. His son, Jesus, took our punishment for anything we have done wrong; He served our sentence for us. Why? Because He loves us that much. The world and our own self-deprecating thoughts want to keep us in the bondage of guilt, shame, and pride. He wants us to accept His love and grace and experience freedom in them. That is only possible if we choose to believe what God says about us and not the world. God and His grace say we are forgiven.

In turn, we are called to extend that love and grace to others, not condemn, chastise, or even inflate them but give them grace and have mercy on them. Ephesians 4:2 (NLT) says, "Be humble and gentle. Be patient with each other, making allowance for each other's faults because of your love." This can be so difficult, even seemingly impossible at times. The truth is people are capable of such cruel and hurtful things. It makes it difficult to have mercy on them and forgive. Colossians 3:13 (ESV) says, "Bearing with one another and, if one has a complaint against another, forgiving each other; as the Lord has forgiven you, so you also must forgive." There are many other passages that say similar things. It is clear that God wants us to love others by forgiving them. On our own, we may not be able, but with His help, we can.

THE BEST I CAN WITH WHAT I HAVE

So many times, I have heard people say they can't forgive someone because that person doesn't deserve forgiveness. Or they believe forgiving them would be like saying what they did was somehow permissible. This is not the case. God loves us. We have already established that. He does not approve of others hurting or mistreating His children. Forgiving someone is much more about surrendering the situation to God and allowing Him to handle the injustice. Having a spirit of unforgiveness keeps us trapped. We can become consumed with grief, bitterness, anger, etc. This can pour out into many areas of our lives, negatively affecting other relationships. Unforgiveness continues to let our enemies cause us pain without them having to participate at all. Surrendering the person and the situation to God can free us from the control that this spirit of unforgiveness can have on us. He is more than capable of fighting the battle for us.

Giving grace and mercy to others and loving them the way we should is a process. This process isn't always easy or fast. Loving and forgiving ourselves isn't easy either. God didn't give us stories in the Bible of perfect people behaving perfectly. He used broken, sinful, ill-equipped people to do things they couldn't have done on their own. These stories give us hope for our own lives. They remind us that when we surrender to God's will, we are capable of playing our songs beautifully and in tune. We were created with a purpose. We have our own part in His orchestra, meant to be experienced in perfect harmony with others, to produce a wonderful masterpiece, enjoyed by God Himself.

Remember, God doesn't call us to perfection, He calls us to do our best. He asks that we are humble enough to admit our mistakes and try to learn from them. He asks us to love the people He has placed in our path the best we know how, and He asks us to seek and trust Him to fill in the gaps and be willing to be used for His Kingdom and glory.

REFERENCES

1. *Bible Gateway, including English Standard Version (ESV), New International Version (NIV), King James Version, New Living Translation (NLT), and the Message Translation.* 2008. Harper Collins Christian Publishing. biblegateway.com.
2. Meisner, Bob, and Audrey Meisner. 2017. *My Personality Goals.* lovemarriedlife.com
3. Good Reads. 2007. "Theodore Roosevelt Quotes." goodreads.com.

ABOUT THE AUTHOR

Heather has an intense passion for helping people overcome life's difficulties by pointing them toward God's perspective and allowing Him to drive change and growth within them. It is serving this passion that has led her to pursue and finish her master's degree in biblical counseling. Heather has been married to her husband, Brian, for twenty-seven years, and they have five wonderful children together. This passion has also led her, along with her husband, to start and lead a marriage ministry at her church in the Phoenix, Arizona, area.